This book belongs to: Joseph Sagara

Dedicated to McKinley Goolsby, my nephews, and everyone this book represents.

Change the World, you were meant for it.

Aa

is for

Silas

Adekunle

A boy like me who holds technology dear, that's why he's the highest paid robotics engineer

The first boy like me to be president of the USA, history was made on his inauguration day

Bb

is for

Barack

Obama

Cc

is for

Cullen

Jones

The first boy like me to hold a world record in swimming, When he's underwater you can bet he's winning

The first boy like me to drive full-time, in a NASCAR cup series since Wendell in his prime

Dd
is for
Darrell
Wallace Jr.

Ee

is for

Edward Welburn

A boy like me with plenty car chemistry, to date he's ranked highest in the automobile industry

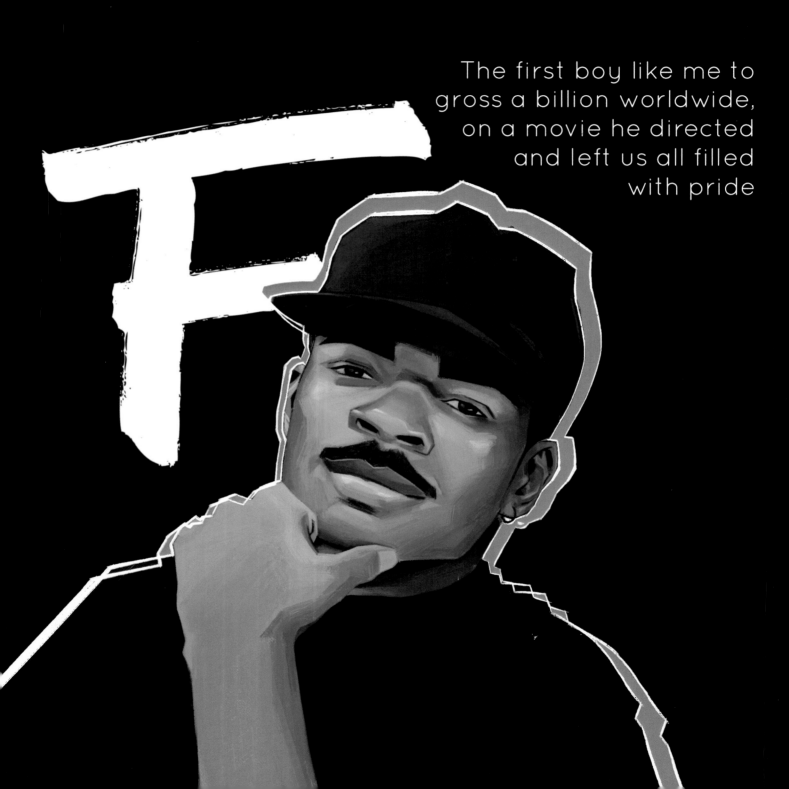

The first boy like me to gross a billion worldwide, on a movie he directed and left us all filled with pride

Ff
is for
Felix

Gary Gray

Gg

is for

Donald

Glover

The first boy like me to win himself an Emmy, for a comedy he directed and representation we saw plenty

He sold out a stadium but he doesn't play ball, the first boy like me to do it while telling jokes for all

Hh

is for

Kevin

Hart

Ii
is for
Barrington Irving

The first boy like me to fly the
world alone, just him and
"inspiration" and
the world he was shown

J

The first boy like me to
win in all four,
Emmy, Grammy, Oscar, Tony,
and he's still doing more.

Jj

is for

John

Legend

Kk

is for

Kendrick Lamar

Beyond his years he is wise,
the first boy like me to rap
and win the Pulitzer prize

He opened a school in his hometown, and as the youngest like me to reach 29,000 points this boy deserves the crown

Ll

is for

LeBron

James

Mm

is for

Michael

Jordan

He started as a NBA player
and now owns a franchise,
the first boy like me to do
both, his legacy
no-one denies

The youngest boy like me to
be a TV writer on staff,
All these years later and
his work still makes us laugh

Nn
is for
Nick
Cannon

Oo

is for
Stanley
O'Neal

The first boy like me to head up a firm, right on Wall Street for a 6 year term

The first boy like me to own a
studio and make movies as a career
From the stage to the big screen,
he brings joy year after year

Pp
is for
Tyler
Perry

Qq

is for

Quincy Jones

The first boy like me to be
a VP and hold the position
at a record company

The first boy like me
to be a billionaire
You can do it too, your
goals you must declare

Rr

is for

Robert

Johnson

is for
terling
Brown

The first boy like me to win a Globe for acting, in a TV drama, now the world he's impacting

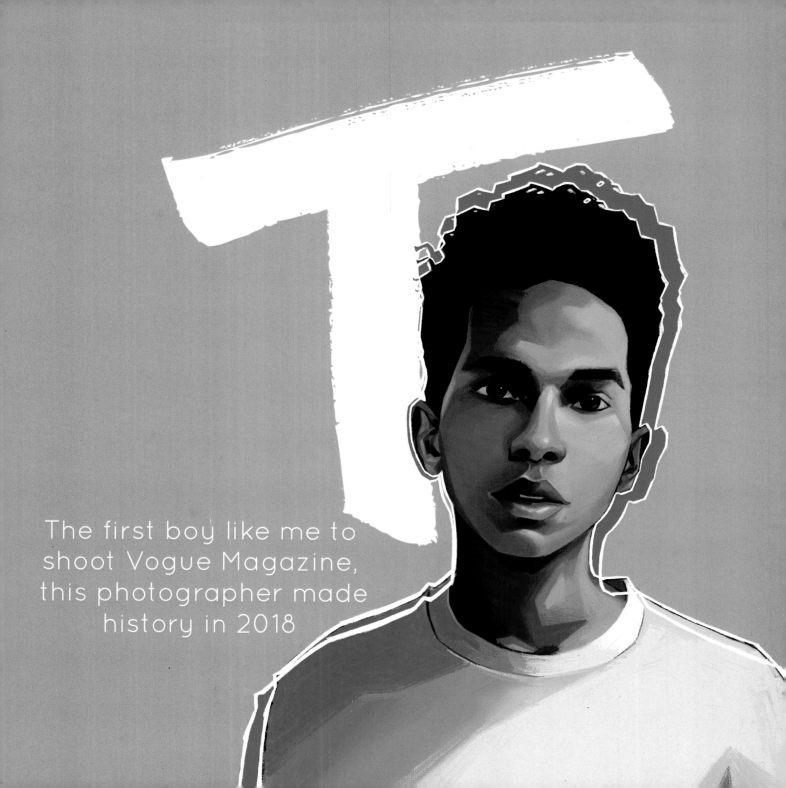

The first boy like me to shoot Vogue Magazine, this photographer made history in 2018

Tt
is for
Tyler
Mitchell

Uu

is for

Usain Bolt

He broke 3 records in a
single olympic game,
you can't talk track & field
without mentioning his name

The first boy like me to be a Louis Vuitton designer, he started at the bottom now he's the headliner

"HOODIE"

Vv

is for

Virgil

Abloh

Ww
is for
Stevie
Wonder

At 13 years old he topped
the billboard charts,
the youngest to do it
with music as his art

2 nominations at the Academy in 1 year, the first boy like me to do it, in this he's a pioneer

Xx

is for

Jamie

Foxx

Yy
is for
Yohan
Blake

He's the youngest to win
the 100 meter dash,
this boy like me
did it in a flash

Yes, he's a rapper
but writing is his game,
for this he's the first to be inducted
in the Songwriters Hall of Fame

Zz

is for

Jay-Z

Now I know my ABCs and 26 boys like you and me!